# FastTrack
## MUSIC INSTRUCTION

# Guitar 2
Electric or Acoustic

MW01040699

# INTRODUCTION

## Why did you buy this book, too?

You bought it because you love learning about the guitar. And we're glad—it's a great instrument!

We assume that you've already completed (and reviewed a couple hundred times) **FastTrack™ Guitar 1**. If not, please consider going through it first. (We'd hate to cover something before you're ready.)

In any case, this book picks up right where **Book 1** ended. You'll learn lots more chords, lots more notes and plenty of cool techniques. And, of course, the last section of all the **FastTrack™** books are the same so that you and your friends can form a band and jam together!

So, if you still feel ready for this book, finish your pizza, put the cat outside, take the phone off the hook, and let's jam…

Always remember the three Ps: **patience**, **practice** and **pace yourself**. We'll add one more to this list: be **proud of yourself** for a job well-done.

# ABOUT THE CD
## (no, it's not a Frisbee!)

**W**e're glad you noticed the added bonus—a CD! Each music example in the book is included on the CD, so you can hear how it sounds and play along when you're ready. Take a listen whenever you see this symbol: ❶

Each example on the CD is preceded by one measure of "clicks" to indicate the tempo and meter. Pan right to hear the guitar part emphasized. Pan left to hear the accompaniment emphasized. As you become more confident, try playing along with the rest of the band. (Remember to use track 1 [❶] on the CD to help you tune before you play.)

**HAL•LEONARD®**
CORPORATION
7777 W. BLUEMOUND RD. P.O. BOX 13819 MILWAUKEE, WI 53213

Copyright © 1997 by HAL LEONARD CORPORATION
International Copyright Secured   All Rights Reserved

No part of this publication may be reproduced in any form or by any means without the prior written permission of the Publisher.

Visit Hal Leonard online at
www.halleonard.com

# LESSON 1

## *The power to move!*

Let's begin with something fun and easy—more power chords! A power chord is one of the most common components of rock and pop guitar playing. So, let's get started...

### Movable Power Chord Shapes

In **Book 1**, we learned three two-note power chords: E5, A5 and D5. Using the new power chords introduced below, you'll be able to play the rest! That sounds like a lot, but the basic shapes below are **movable**. That is, you can use the same hand position and move up and down the neck of your guitar to play many, many more power chords. Here's how...

Look at the photos and diagrams below. For now, it doesn't matter which fret you begin on. Simply observe the two- and three-note shapes and their respective **roots** (lowest strings):

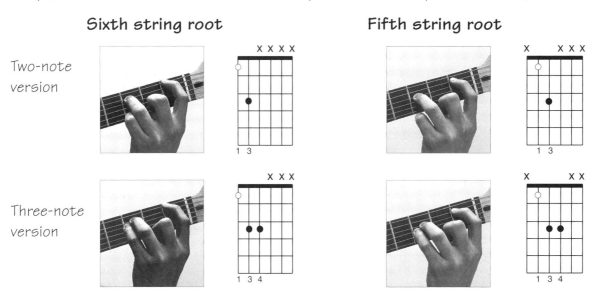

OPTIONS: Choose either the two- or three-note version. Both are essentially the same chord, so use whichever sounds better or feels more comfortable to you.

### Give it a name...

A power chord is named by its root note; the suffix used is "5." If you want to play C5, locate C on either string 6 or string 5 and apply the correct shape from above. Move to D5 by simply sliding up two frets. That's the logic behind **movable chords**.

The fingerboard chart below gives you all the notes on the first twelve frets of strings 5 and 6:

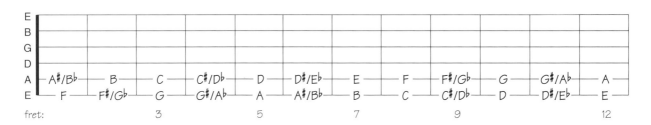

## Get a grasp...

To make sure you understand all this "movable" stuff, we'll explain a bit further. Take a look at the chords below, paying special attention to their given names and root positions.

| Chord | Root String | Root Fret | Diagram |
|-------|-------------|-----------|---------|
| F5 | 6 | 1 | x x x  1 3 4 |
| G5 | 6 | 3 | x x x  1 3 4 |
| A5 | 6 or 5 | 5 or open | x x x  5 fr  1 3 4  or  x ○ x x  3 4 |
| B♭5 | 5 or 6 | 1 or 6 | x x x  1 3 4  or  x x x  6 fr  1 3 4 |

## Let's jam!

FRIENDLY TIP: Make sure you only play the strings your left hand is pressing. And one more thing—turn it up!

### ◆2 Take the Stage

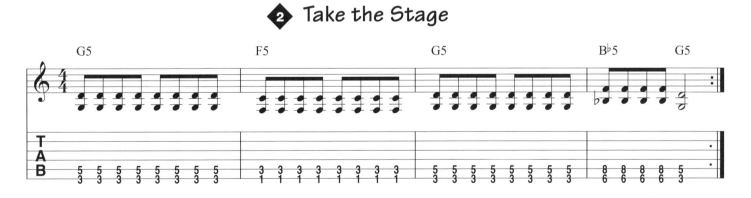

☞ Avoid cramping by releasing the left-hand pressure slightly
as you slide from one power chord to the next.

*Now try a few that change between strings 5 and 6...*

### ❸ It Used to be Mine

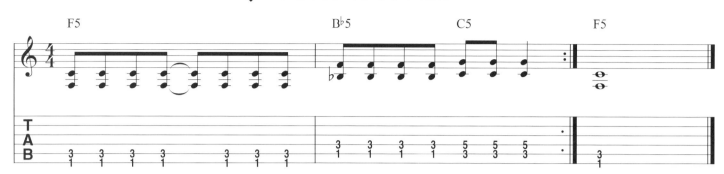

### ◆ '50s Pop

### ❺ Rock All Night

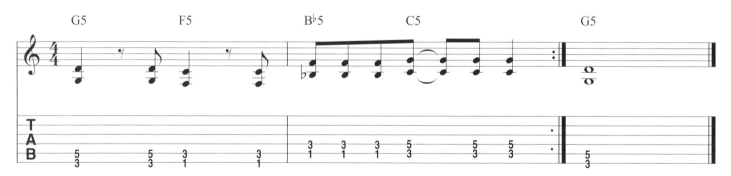

### ❻ Sweet and Low

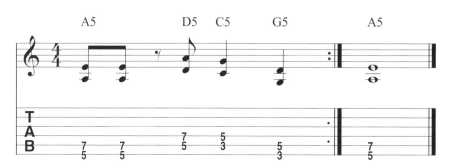

You've got the hang of it, so let's take the next one a little faster! Play the three-note shapes on this one...

### 7 Alternative Guitar

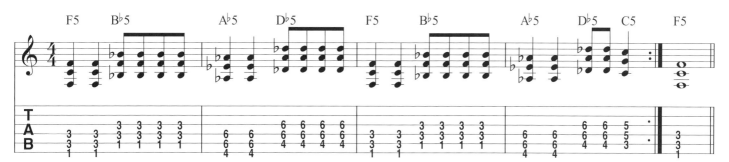

**Palm Muting**

**Palm muting** means to use the heel of your picking hand to muffle (or "mute") the strings. Use this technique when you see the abbreviation P.M. under the notes (between the staff and the TAB). You'll notice a thicker, more percussive sound as you play.

Palm muting sounds REALLY cool with power chords and some **distortion.** (If you don't have an electric guitar or a distortion pedal—no problem! It's still a cool sound.) Let's try it loud...

### 8 Muted Groove

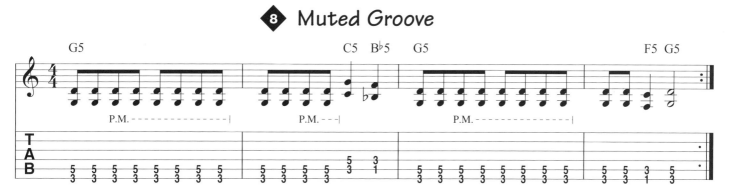

An **accent mark** (>) written above or below a note means exactly what it sounds like—accent it! That is, play the note or chord slightly louder than the others.

### 9 Summer Lovin'

# A BIT FASTER NOW

What if you want to play faster than eighth notes but in the same tempo? Welcome to the world of sixteenths.

## Sixteenth Notes

These have two flags or beams: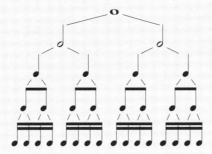

Sixteenth rests look like eighth rests but with two flags: 𝄿

## Yuck, more math...

Two sixteenths equal one eighth (just like fractions), and four sixteenths equal one quarter. Here's a diagram showing the relationship of all the rhythmic values you've learned:

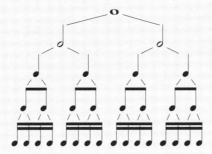

To count sixteenths, divide the beat into four by counting "1 e & a, 2 e & a, 3 e & a, 4 e & a":

1 e & a  2 e & a  3 e & a  4 e & a

Listen to Track 10 on the CD (with steady quarter note clicks throughout) to hear this new faster rhythm.

## ❿ Progressively Faster

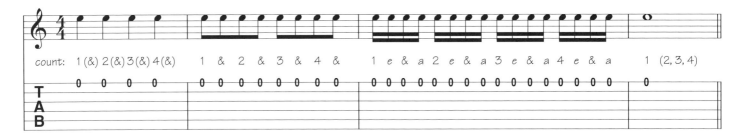

Now try playing it. Remember to play slowly at first and speed up the tempo only as it becomes easier.

That's a little hard on the right hand, huh? EASY SOLUTION: alternate downstrokes (⊓) and upstrokes (V) on the next example.

## ⑪ An Alternate Way

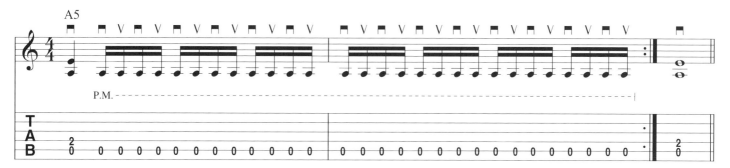

Try sixteenths with two of your power chords...

## ⑫ Power Sixteenths

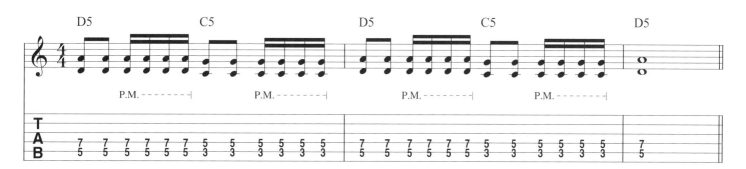

Of course, you can apply the sixteenth rhythm to all six strings. Try out your down-stroke/upstroke pattern with a few full chords from Book 1:

## ⑬ Sixteenth Strumming

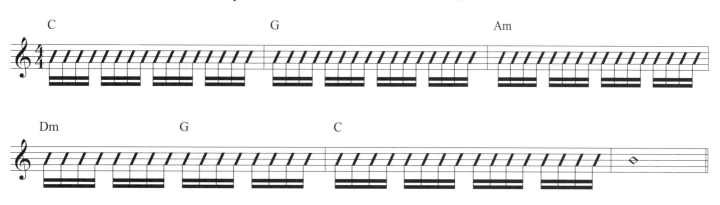

☞    We like to encourage breaks on a regular basis, and this is no exception.
Take five and we'll see you back here for Lesson 2.

# LESSON 2
## *Guitars were made for strumming...*

In Book 1, you learned several **open chords** (chords that contain some open strings): C, G, D, Em, Am and Dm. Open chords are the most fundamental chords to all styles of guitar playing. So, what do you say to learning some new ones?

### New Chords: E and A

These two are easy, but they stretch a little—be patient...

This one is similar to Em, but we include fret 1 on string 3:

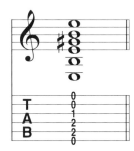

Your fingers may feel sort of crowded on this one.

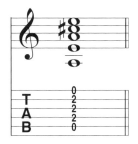

EASY OPTION: If your fingers feel too crowded on the A chord, consider an option many rock players use—flatten finger 1 across strings 1-4 and don't strum string 1.

Try out your new chords with some old ones:

### 14 Strum Along

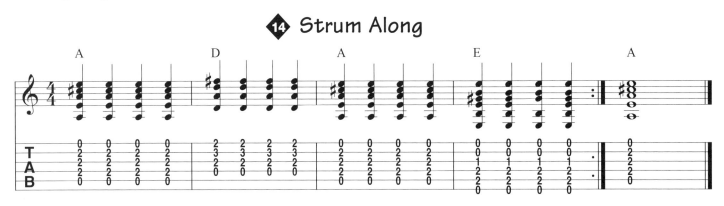

Want to look up even more chords?
☞ Buy **FastTrack™ Guitar Chords & Scales**, an excellent supplement book with over 1,400 chord diagrams and much more.

8

When playing chords, it's a good idea to vary your strum pattern. But let's not get ahead of ourselves—we'll start with a few common (and easy) strumming patterns. Pay close attention to the stroke indications (⊓ and V).

**Strum pattern #1**

This one works great with almost any tempo.
Apply it to the chord progression in track 15.

### 15 Strum, Strum, Strum!

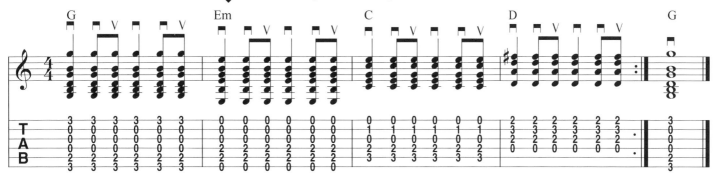

**Strum pattern #2**

Try this one with medium to faster tempo songs.
Listen to track 16 to get the feel.

### 16 Acoustic Rock

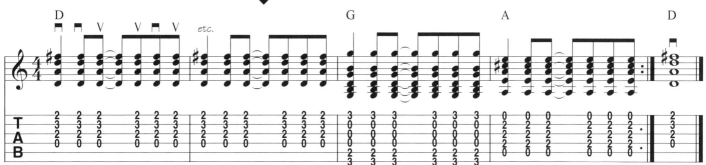

**Strum pattern #3**

This one uses sixteenth notes, so be careful with the counting.
It works best with a slower tempo like that in track 17.

### 17 Acoustic Ballad

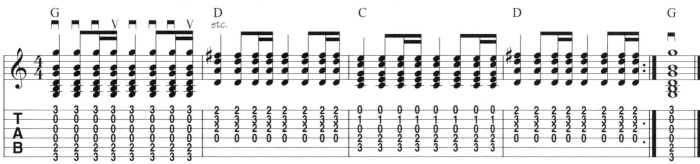

9

**Strum pattern #4**

Let's not forget 3/4 meter.
Take your pick—they both work fine.

### 🔸18 1-2-3 Strum

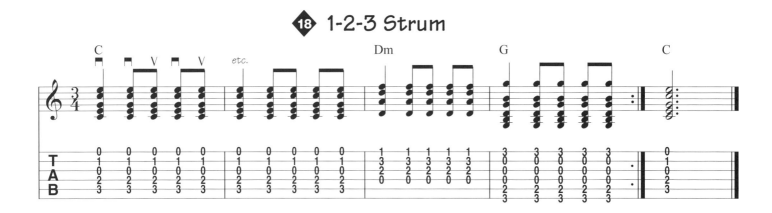

## Mixing it up...

Notice how the strumming pattern changes in the next example. (Pay close attention to the downstroke and upstroke markings.)

### 🔸19 That's What I Like

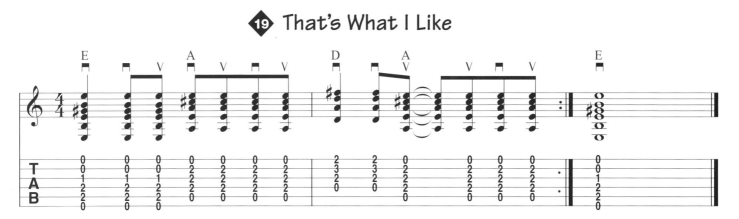

# MORE MUTING

Instead of palm muting, try simply **releasing the left-hand pressure** as you strum the chords. Notice the muffled, percussive sound. This may feel tricky at first, but practice with patience.

NOTE: The "X" in both the notation and TAB tell you when to apply muting.

### 🔸20 Mute This!

Now that you have the hang of strumming, let's add another chord—F major. All along, we've said to arch your fingers when playing chords. Well, it's time to break the rules...

## New Chord: F

F major requires a new technique—the use of a **barre** (pronounced like "bar"). Barring is done by flattening the specified finger on more than one string at a time.

 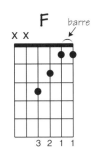

Flatten finger 1 across strings 1 and 2 at the same time and place fingers 2 and 3 in their proper places.

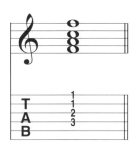

CAREFUL: Make sure you're pressing evenly and firmly with the barre finger. If the chord sounds bad, play each string one at a time to determine which string isn't being barred correctly.

**21 Guitar Twang**

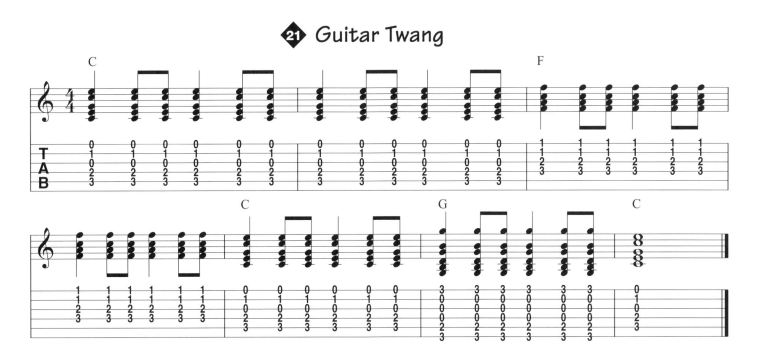

The barring technique comes in very handy throughout your guitar-playing career (especially when we get to Lesson 7), so practice this until it becomes almost second nature.

**22 Dark Rock**

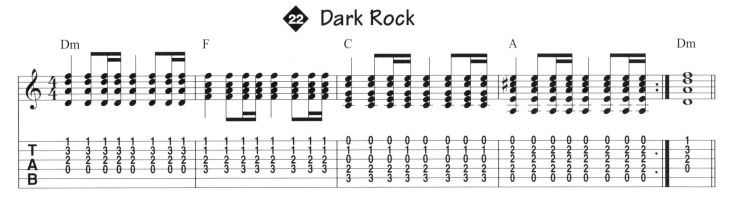

# IF IT AIN'T BROKE...BREAK IT!

Guitarists often prefer to play **broken chords** rather than strum. A broken chord (or "arpeggio," if you prefer the Italian word) offers a lighter accompaniment and works nicely with ballads.

The next example uses the same chord progression as track 21 from the previous page. But this time use the broken chord technique.

## 23 Breakin' Up Ain't Hard to Do

PLAYING TIP: You don't really have to look at the notation. Simply follow the chord symbols and play the strings of the chord one at a time up and then down.

Easy enough? Now mix some broken chords with some full-strummed chords...

## 24 Hey, Jim

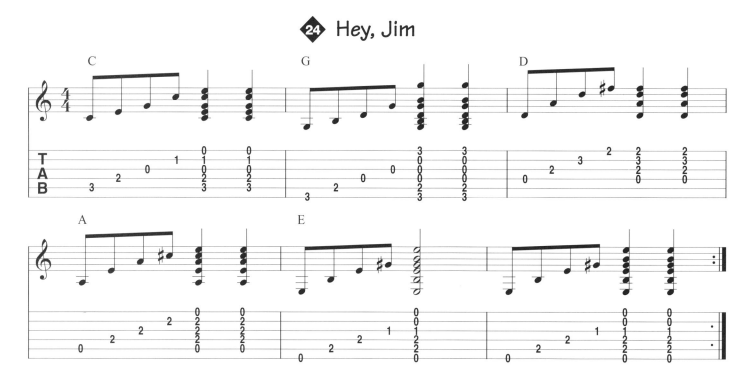

12

# LESSON 3
## *Back to the basics...*

Very briefly, let's take some time to review the note positions we learned in Book 1 (and add some finishing touches)...

### First Position Review

The area of the guitar neck from the open strings to fret 4 is called **first position**. The diagram and note chart below cover all of the notes in this area.

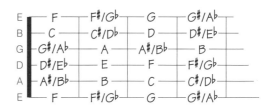

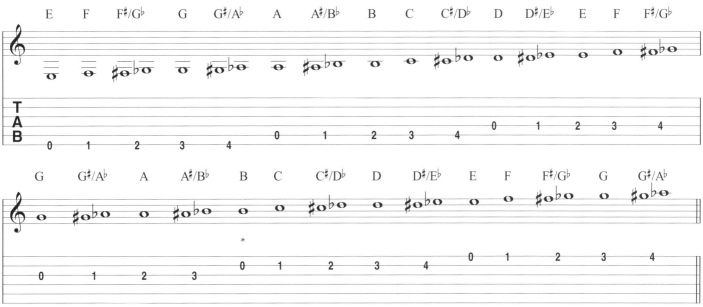

*this note can also be played on the third string, fourth fret

IMPORTANT: Some notes can have different names but occupy the same fret (for example, F# and Gb). These are referred to as **enharmonic equivalents**. Either spelling is acceptable.

Let's try some songs using the notes from first position...

### 25 Deuces

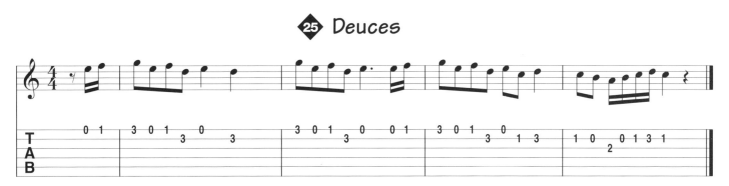

13

## ◈26 Für Elise

## ◈27 Boogie Woogie

*We knew you'd ace this Lesson, so here's a treat—a new kind of rhythm...*

# EVERYTHING AND THE KITCHEN SYNC

Let's take a minute to learn one of the most essential (and fun) rhythmic concepts in music...

## Syncopation

Syncopation is simply playing notes "off the beat." It makes the music sound less predictable (and, hey, it's great to dance to). Listen to a non-syncopated example on the CD:

### 28 Not Quite

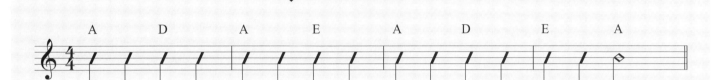

Now, listen to the same example with syncopation:

### 29 Just Right

You can still feel the beat, but it certainly has a hipper groove to it.

This bluesy ditty has plenty of syncopation.

### 30 In Sync

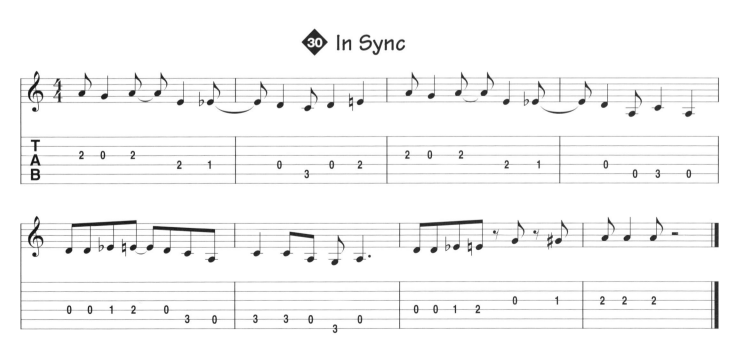

The next song has a **1st and 2nd ending** (indicated by brackets and the number "1" and "2").
Play the song once to the repeat sign (1st ending), then repeat from measure 2. The second
time through, skip the 1st ending and play the 2nd (last) ending.

## 31 The Entertainer

☞ Time for another break.
Do something that doesn't involve counting—you know, like your taxes or something?!

# LESSON 4
## *Keys, please...*

A song's key is determined by the scale used to create the song. For example, a song based on the C major scale is said to be in the key of C. Since learning about keys requires a good knowledge of scales, let's learn more about just that—scales!

## What's in a name?

Two things give a scale its name: the scale's **root note** (the lowest note, just like with power chords) and the **pattern** of whole steps and half steps used. (REMINDER: from one fret to the next on your guitar equals one half step.)

Here's a look at the two most important scale patterns:

### Major Scale Pattern

NOTE: The root note is C here, so it is the C major scale.

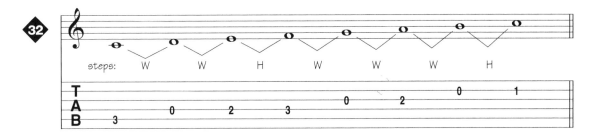

### Minor Scale Pattern

NOTE: Although the root is the same (C), the different step pattern makes this a C minor scale.

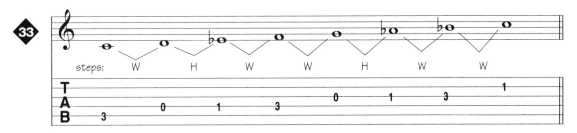

LEARN IT BY EAR: Without checking the pattern, you can hear the difference between a major and minor scale. Like chords, a major scale sounds "happy;" a minor scale sounds "sad."

## Sharps and flats are unavoidable...

Depending on the root note used, most scales contain sharps or flats. (There are two exceptions: **C major** and **A minor** have no sharps or flats.) Since keys and scales are related, a key will have the same number of sharps or flats as its corresponding scale.

## Sign in, please...

A **key signature** is used at the beginning of each line of music to tell you two important things:

 Notes to play sharp or flat throughout the piece

 Song's key

For example, the key of G contains F#, so its key signature will have one sharp on the F-line. This tells you to play all Fs as F# (unless, of course, you see a natural sign ♮).

Here are some common scales and keys...

### Key of C

Based on the C major scale, which has no sharps or flats:

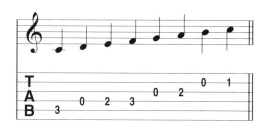

## 34 I've Been Rocking on the Railroad

NOTE: The key of C looks like there is no key signature, since there are no sharps or flats.

## Key of G

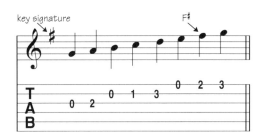

Based on the G major scale, which has one sharp—F#:

### 35 Jamaica Farewell

## Key of F

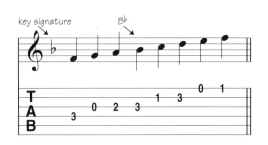

Based on the (you guessed it!) F major scale, which has one flat—B♭:

### 36 America

Enhance your new knowledge of keys with a new type of chord—a **dominant seventh chord**.

## New Chords: Dominant 7ths

There are three categories of chords: **major**, **minor** and **dominant**. With these three categories you can play nearly any pop or rock song. Here are a few common dominant seventh "open" chords...

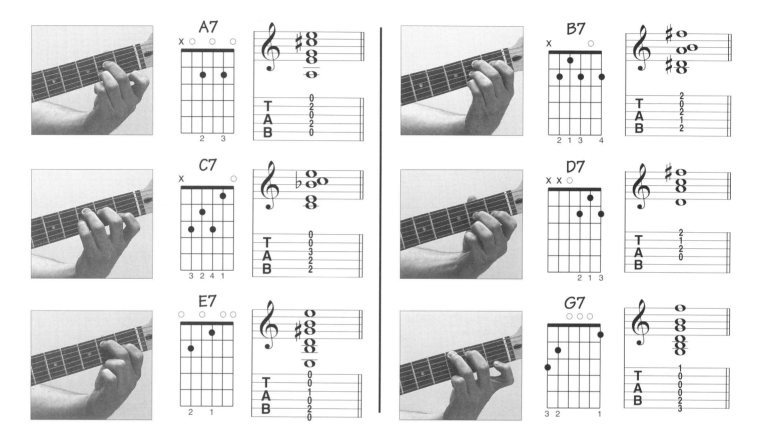

Track 37 is a comparison of a G major and G7 (dominant) chord:

**37** *G–G7*

Notice how the G7 sounds "unresolved?" A dominant chord adds a bit of musical "tension" and makes the ear want musical "relief." This relief can come from a major or minor chord played after the dominant chord, like in the last two measures of the next example:

**38** Seventh Heaven

Or you can play songs that sort of "leave you hanging" by never resolving the dominant chord:

**39 Bluesy Sevenths**

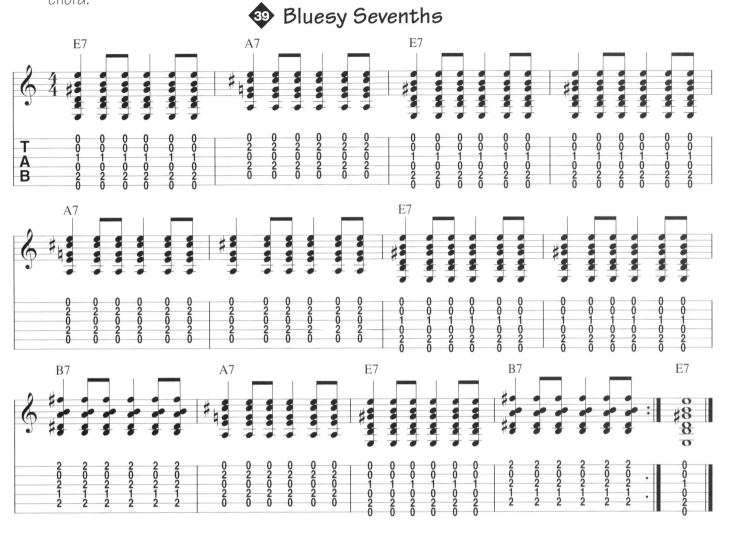

**40 Ragtime Rhythm**

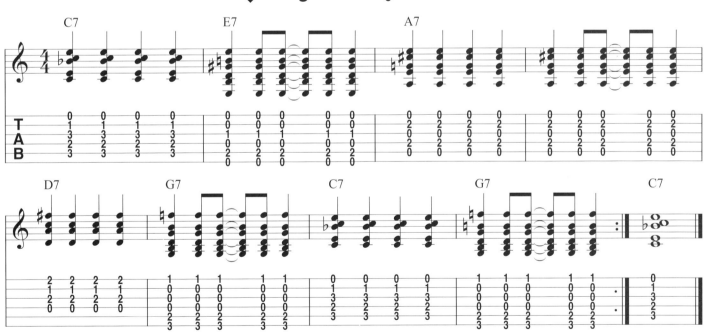

REMINDER: For more scales Sevends and dominant chords, buy
*FastTrack*™ **Guitar Chords & Scales**. It's an excellent supplement book
with an in-depth look at what we introduced in this Lesson.

# LESSON 5
## *You've got the blues...*

If you haven't heard of the **blues,** then where have you been? It's been around for ages and has been used by such music legends as B.B. King, Eric Clapton, and Muddy Waters. Blues is fun (and easy) to play.

### 12-Bar Form

The most typical blues uses a form called **12-bar form**. This doesn't mean that the song is only twelve bars (measures) long. Rather, the song uses several 12-bar phrases (or sections) repeated over and over.

Generally, blues songs use only three chords: the **first, fourth,** and **fifth** chords of the key (indicated with Roman numerals I, IV and V). To find these three chords, count up the scale from the root of the key:

| Key | Chord / Scale Tone | | | | | | | |
|---|---|---|---|---|---|---|---|---|
| | I | | | IV | V | | | |
| Blues in "C" | C | D | E | F | G | A | B | C |
| Blues in "F" | F | G | A | B♭ | C | D | E | F |
| Blues in "G" | G | A | B | C | D | E | F♯ | G |
| Blues in "D" | D | E | F♯ | G | A | B | C♯ | D |

Listen to the following example of 12-bar blues in "G" on Track 41. Then strum along...

### 🔶41 Blues in G

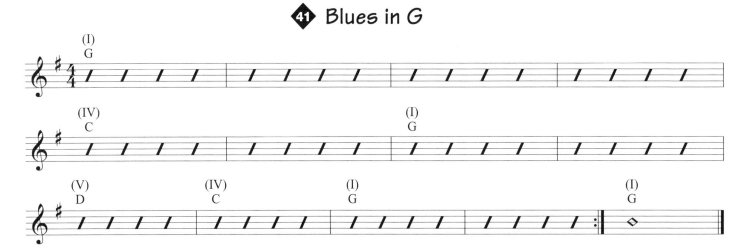

IMPORTANT: Notice the number of measures each chord is played during the 12-bar form. This is the most common 12-bar blues chord progression...

| Chord | | Measures |
|---|---|---|
| I | = | four |
| IV | = | two |
| I | = | two |
| V | = | one |
| IV | = | one |
| I | = | two |

## Turnaround, sit up, and play...

The last two bars of the 12-bar blues progression are sometimes called the **turnaround,** since it "turns" the form back "around" to the beginning. Musicians often vary the turnaround, using different chords or even a written out riff.

The most common turnaround variation uses the V chord in the last measure like in the example below:

### 42 The Sky Is Whining

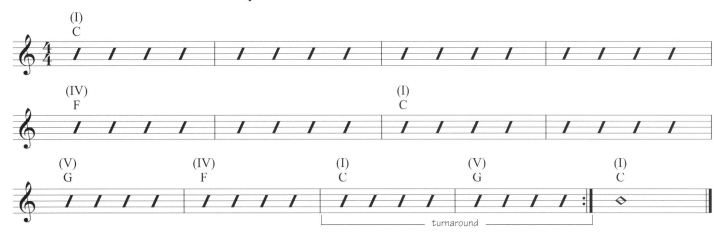

Minor chords and seventh chords are also very popular in blues progressions...

### 43 Minor Blues

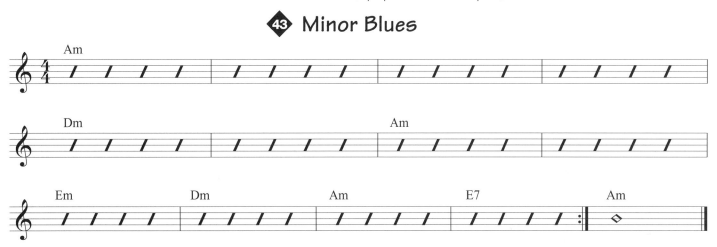

Another variation is to play the IV chord in measure 2. This is called the **quick change,** since you "change" to the IV and "quickly" return to the I.

### 44 Quick Change Artist

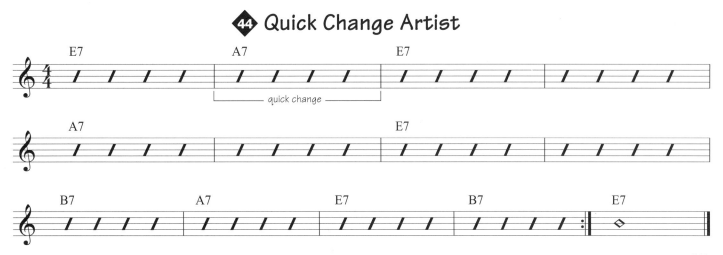

Track 45 employs another popular blues rhythm accompaniment. Chuck Berry and other early rock 'n' roll players used this "back and forth" rhythm extensively.

## 45 Rock 'n' Roll Rhythm

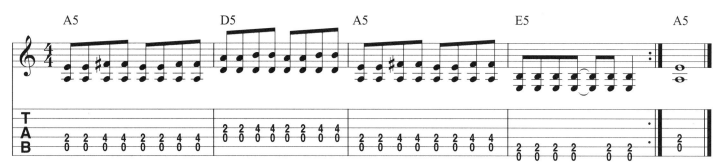

## Just add the pinkie...

The rhythm you just played can be applied to power chords very easily. Play the power chord, then keep your fingers in the same shape and add your pinkie (finger 4) two frets above your third finger. This will take a little stretching, but it's worth it.

HELPFUL TIP: If you're having problems making the stretch, try moving your wrist further beneath the guitar neck (shown in the photo).

## 46 Rockin' and Compin'

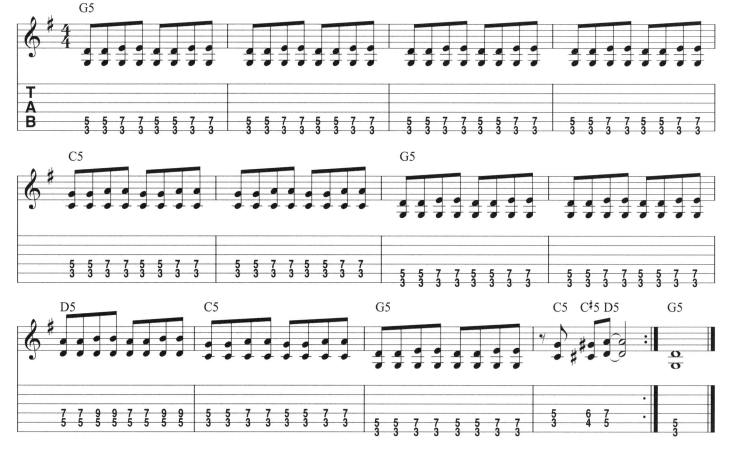

If you want to spice up a blues jam, try soloing over the 12-bar section using notes from the blues scale.

## Blues Scale

This scale is popular in rock, jazz, and (you guessed it) blues music. First observe the scale's step pattern, then learn its fretboard pattern.

**Blues scale (F as root)**

**Movable fretboard pattern**
o = root

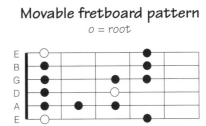

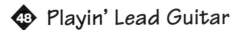

steps:　W + H　　W　　H　　H　　W + H　　W

As with the major and minor scales you learned, the blues scale pattern can be used on any root note. Commit this pattern to memory and use it to form some great riffs and solos like this next one:

## 🔶 Playin' Lead Guitar

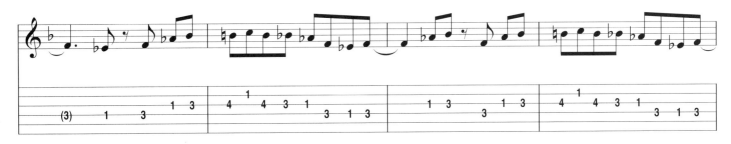

👉 **W**hen playing the blues, almost any note sounds good, so don't worry if you play a wrong note occasionally.

# SHUT UP AND SHUFFLE!

The **shuffle feel** is a very common element of rock, blues, pop and jazz music. It uses a new rhythmic value called a **triplet**.

## Triplets

By now you know that two eighth notes equal one quarter, and four eighth notes equal one half. Guess what? Three eighth notes played in the duration of one beat (or one quarter note) is an **eighth-note triplet**.

A triplet is beamed together with a number 3:

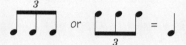

To count a triplet, simply say the word "tri-pl-et" during one beat. Tap your foot to the beat and count out loud as you listen to track 49:

Here's a perfect example of triplets used in a well-known classical piece. Keep tapping your foot as you listen to and follow the song:

Now play it yourself. Keep thinking "tri-pl-et, tri-pl-et, tri-pl-et, tri-pl-et" as you tap your foot to the beat...

You can also use the word "cho-co-late" to help you count triplets. (Of course, this could make you really hungry after counting a long song?!)

26

Moving up a few centuries in music, let's play some triplets in a rock-style shuffle:

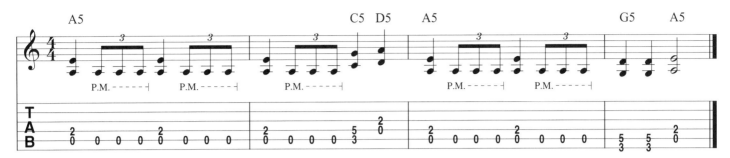

**51** **Three of a Kind**

Triplets can also include rests. Most common is to have a rest within the triplet (between two eighth notes):

**52**

Once you get the hang of this "bouncy" feel, you'll never forget it...

**53** **Berry-like**

# 3/4, 4/4, 12/8?

Until this page, you've been playing with time signatures in which the quarter note equals one beat. Let's learn something new (change is good!):

12 beats per measure
eighth note (1/8) = one beat

All notes and rests are relative to the value of an eighth note in 12/8 meter:

eighth = one beat      quarter = two beats      dotted quarter = three beats

In 12/8 meter, an eighth note equals one beat and there are twelve beats per measure. But the rhythmic **pulse** feels like there are only four beats per measure. Listen and count along to track 54, and you'll see what we mean:

count:  1  2  3,  4  5  6  (7  8)  9,  10  11  12

Now try a few riffs in your new meter...

## 55 Delta Blues

## 56 Berry-like in 12/8

 LISTEN AND COMPARE: The rhythmic feel of track 56 and track 53 (on the previous page) sound the same. That's because 12/8 meter is divided into groups of three, just like triplets in 4/4 meter.

# LESSON 6

## *A little bit higher...*

In Lesson 3 we reviewed all the notes in first position. Of course, not every song can be played down there, so let's learn some higher notes...

### Fifth Position

Except for the power chords, you've been playing mostly on the first four frets. To play notes above fret 4 requires sliding up to **fifth position**, aptly named because you move up to the fifth fret.

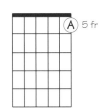

Slide your hand up the guitar neck and place finger 1 on fret 5 to play high A.

NOTE: To help you quickly find this position, you'll notice a little white dot at fret 5 on your guitar neck. It's easier than counting, right?

Take a few minutes now to review the diagram and exercise below. Make sure you spend time learning where the notes are on both the fretboard and the staff. (Tell your fingers what you're playing—say each note out loud as you press it.)

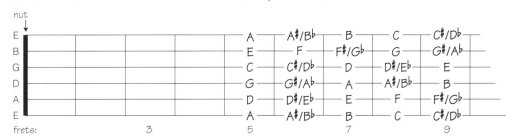

### 🔊57 Fifth Position Chromatics

To get a better grip on this new position, try a few scales…

## 58 Two-octave C Major Scale

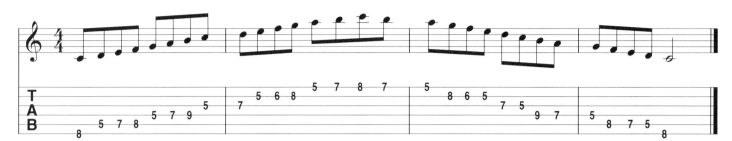

## 59 Two-octave A Minor Scale

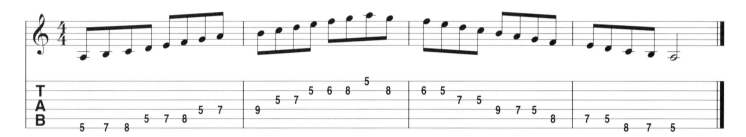

Scales are good exercises, but riffs sound great up here, too…

## 60 Water Chestnut

The next one uses an open string (low E) while your left hand stays in fifth position for the rest of the riff:

## 61 Zodiak

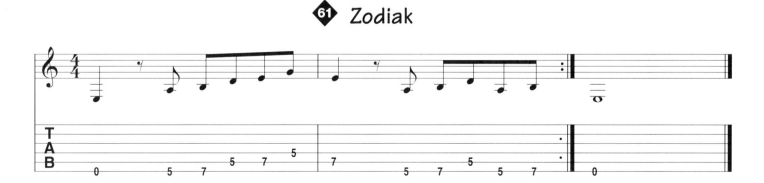

When you think you know the new notes well enough, try some songs. (IMPORTANT: Use only fifth position notes—don't slide back to open position on these songs.)

## 62 Shenandoah

## 63 Oh, Susannah

Keep it slow and fun, so you don't get frustrated!

## When to change...

Generally speaking, if you're going to play up high for a while, stay in fifth position. Too much unnecessary sliding will tire you out (and sound clumsy).

If you don't have TAB to show you the convenient positions to play a song, it's a good idea to survey each song before you play and mark appropriate spots to change positions. Players often use Roman numerals (I and V) to mark these spots—in fact, so do we...

### 64 Arkansas Traveler

## Squeaky clean...

You may notice your hand making a little "squeaking" sound as you move between positions. Don't worry about it. In fact, you'll notice this sound is pretty common in almost all guitar recordings. (But don't cause a blister—release left-hand pressure as you move between positions.)

Take a break—call a friend and have them learn another **FastTrack**™ instrument. But don't dial too fast...you're supposed to rest those fingers!

# LESSON 7
## *Grin and barre it...*

Remember the barre technique we learned for the F chord on page 11? This technique is used very often. In fact, it will allow you to form **movable barre chords**, so you can play all around the neck with your fingers in the same shape.

### "E" Type Barre Chord

By definition, barre chords are chords in which two or more strings are depressed using the same finger. In general, there are two types of barre chords: those with their root on string 6 and those with their root on string 5. (Sound familiar? That's right—just like power chords!)

Forming a barre chord is a three-step process, so hang in there...

 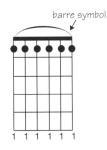

STEP ONE: Flatten finger 1 and barre all six strings on the first fret. Strum all six strings and readjust your finger until every string sounds clearly.

STEP TWO: Stop barring and use fingers 3, 4 and 2 to position for an E chord. Smack that chord! (Yes, you're right—normally you'd use fingers 1, 2 and 3 for E, but we need finger 1 for the next step.)

STEP THREE: Now slide this chord shape up to fret 3 and barre fret 1 with finger 1 (as in Step One). Strum all six strings. This is an **F major barre chord**.

Essentially, your new F major barre chord is an E major chord played one fret higher. (Because, as you know, one fret higher than E is F.) Therefore, some players refer to this chord shape as the **"E" type barre chord**.

Need a little help?
Turn finger 1 slightly to the side when using it to barre, as in the photos above.

Give your new barre chord a whirl with track 65:

### ◆65 The Corner Barre

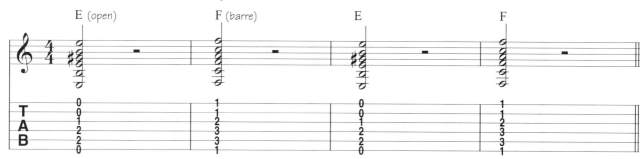

## "Em" Type Barre Chord

The same barring technique can be employed for minor chords, too. We used the E major shape for the major barre chord, so we'll use E minor's shape for the minor ones (makes sense, huh?). Like the major one, this one also uses a sixth string root…

STEP ONE: Just like before, use finger 1 to barre all six strings on fret 1.

STEP TWO: Stop barring and use fingers 3 and 4 to position for an open Em chord. Smack that chord, too!

STEP THREE: Slide the Em shape up one fret and add the barre on fret 1. Play all six strings and hear an **F minor barre chord**.

Now try switching between your two major and minor barre chords. It's as easy as lifting (or adding) finger 2…

### ◆66 All-Holds-Barred

## Movin' on up...

Remember, we said barre chords are **movable**. One fret up from F is F#, so the "E" and "Em" type barre chords moved up one fret from F (so that finger 1 now barres fret 2) produces an F# barre chord. But don't stop there—move up and play G, A♭, A, B♭, etc.

Here's a heavy metal-style tune using your minor barre chord shape, starting with Am (finger 1 barres fret 5)...

 **Mother May I?**

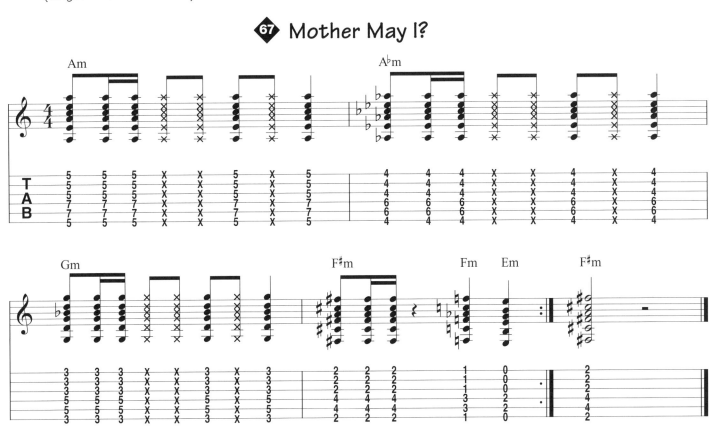

 **TROUBLESHOOTING**

Make sure each string rings out clearly. To check yourself, strike each note in the chord one at a time and determine which string(s) are (accidentally) muted. The cause of the "muted" sound (if any) is usually one of the following:

**1** **String(s) aren't being pressed down hard enough.**
SOLUTION: Use leverage from both your fingers and thumb to press down harder.

**2** **Part of one finger is blocking an adjacent string.**
SOLUTION: Readjust your wrist further under the neck to arch your fingers (all except finger 1).

Just as you converted the E and Em chord shapes into barre chord shapes, do the same thing with A and Am chord shapes...

## "A" Type Barre Chord

This barre chord shape uses a fifth string root (so don't play string 6).

Open A chord shape...          ...converted barre chord shape

Instead of squeezing your fingers together on the fretted notes, just make another barre by **bending the knuckle** (ouch!) of finger 3 and laying it across strings 2-4. (NOTE: If you have difficulty playing string 1, you can leave it out and simply play strings 5-2.)

It may feel awkward for a while, so relax—try barring with finger 3 by itself and add finger 1 later when it feels more comfortable. (Hey, no pain...no gain!)

## "Am" Type Barre Chord

Another fifth string root. Notice how it looks just like the "E" type barre chord but moved over one string.

Open Am chord shape...          ...converted barre chord shape

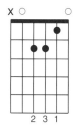  

RELAX: Barre chords aren't that easy! Sometimes barre chords take weeks of practice, so be patient. Just relax and keep working 'em.

One fret higher than A is B-flat, so your new barre chords are B♭ and B♭m, respectively. Try 'em out...

### 68 Just B(e) Flat

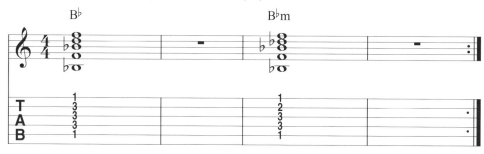

Here's an exercise combining all four barre chord shapes you just learned. Take it slow!

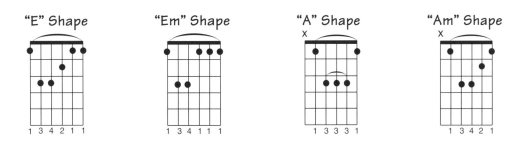

"E" Shape    "Em" Shape    "A" Shape    "Am" Shape

69 Barre Exam

## Keep it moving...

Don't forget—barre chords are cool 'cause they're **movable**. Move all four shapes anywhere on the fingerboard to produce a new chord name at each new fret location.

IMPORTANT: Pay special attention to which string (fifth or sixth) the root is on, and which quality (major or minor) that barre shape yields.

## GAME BREAK: NAME THAT CHORD!

Use the chart below to help you locate the roots and name each chord below:

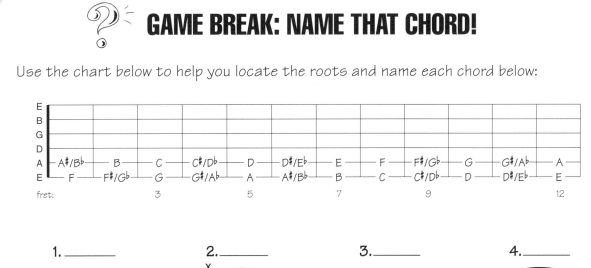

1. _____  2. _____  3. _____  4. _____

  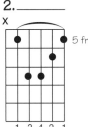  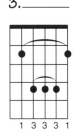  

ANSWERS: 1. G, 2. Dm, 3. B, 4. Dm

You've been patient, so here are two full pages of songs and riffs with barre chords…

## 🔷70 If It Moves You

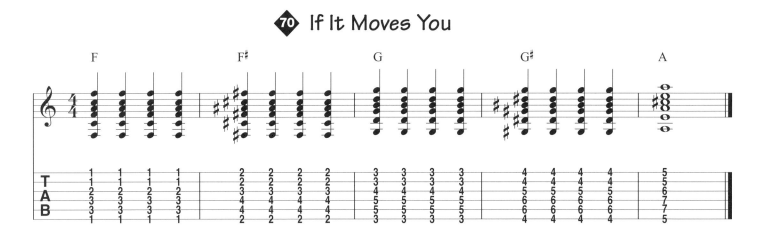

## 🔷71 All Along the Sidewalk

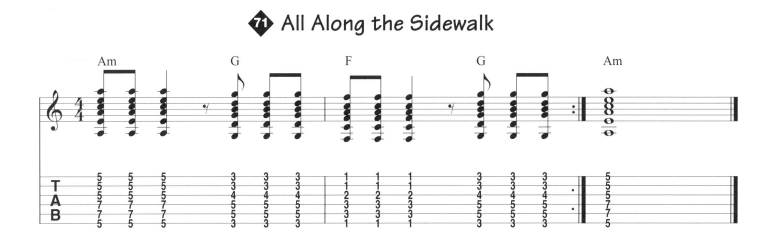

IMPORTANT: As you play up and down the neck, say out loud the name of the chord. You'll begin to remember which neck position produces which chord.

## 🔷72 Coconuts

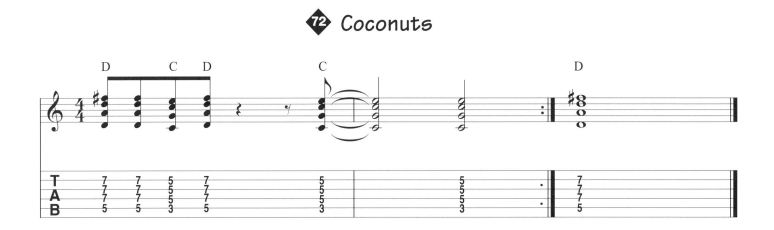

DON'T COUNT: Use the white dots on the guitar neck to help you locate the higher frets quickly.

## 73 Livin' After Dark

PLAYING TIP: Don't allow sliding to interfere with correct barring. Quickly readjust the amount of pressure you're using for the barre after you've slid your hand up. If it sounds bad, press a little harder.

## 74 Punkish

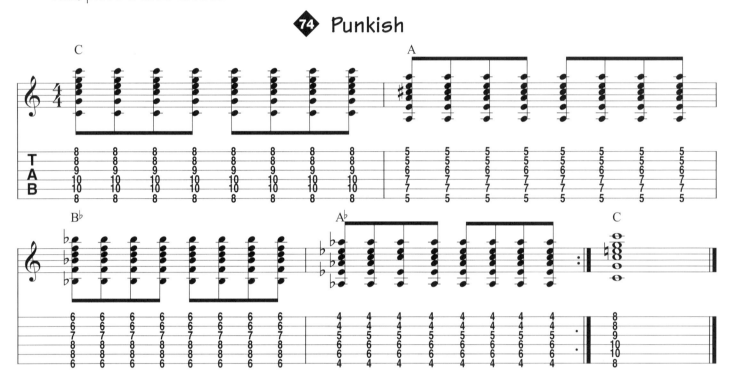

## 75 Dream

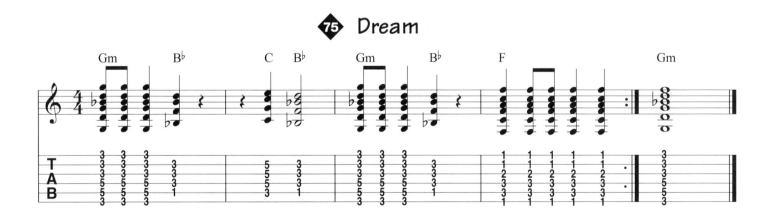

 Time for another break! You owe it to yourself (and to your poor fingers). Knitting would not be a good activity during this break?!

# LESSON 8
## *Let's get fancy...*

**Y**ou've been so patient, learning your chords, notes, and scales. Now's a great time to experiment and learn some "tricks of the trade"—some **slur techniques** that you've probably heard but didn't know how to do.

Slur techniques (or "legato" techniques, if you prefer Italian) allow you to play more than one note for each pick attack. In other words, you'll be able to pick the string once and "slur" two or more notes, giving you a smooth, flowing sound. Here are a few of the most common ones...

### Slide

Looks like this:

Just like it sounds—play the first note by picking the string, then sound the second note by sliding the same finger up or down on the same string. (The second note is not picked!)

Track 76 will give you a good idea of the sound.

Now try using slides in some riffs...

### 77 Up and Back

### 78 Slidin' Chords

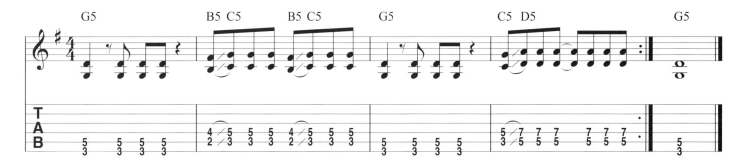

This will take some time to get the hang of, so don't be too hard on yourself.

## Hammer-on

Looks like this:

Again, just like it sounds! The first note is picked, then use another finger as a "hammer" to press down onto the fret of the second (higher) note on the same string.

NOTE: You can only hammer "up" from a lower note to a higher note.

PLAYING TIP: If you hammer too hard, your fingertips will hurt; too soft and you won't hear anything. Practice and practice some more until you think you've got it.

### 80 Frightful

## Pull-off

Looks like this:

This one is the direct opposite of the hammer-on. That is, start with both fingers on their notes, pick the string and then tug or "pull" your higher note finger off the string to sound the lower note.

Now try it in a short riff...

### 82 Push and Pull

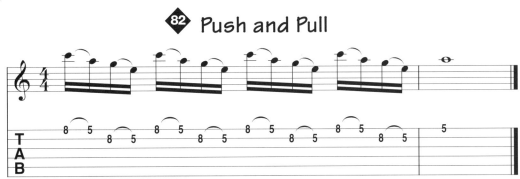

## Bend

Just like it sounds—you're going to raise or "bend" a string to a higher pitch. In general, bending is done on the first three strings, bending up or toward the ceiling.

Most bends are one of the following two types:

 **Whole-step bend**

Pick D on string 3 (fret 7) and push the string upwards to match the sound of the target pitch (E), which is a whole-step higher. (To check yourself, play E on fret 9.)

 **Half-step bend**

 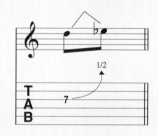

Pick D on string 3 again and push the string not quite as high to match the target pitch (E♭), which is only a half-step higher. (Check yourself this time with fret 8.)

PLAYING TIP: Don't use only your third finger to bend. Add your first and second fingers for extra strength and support. This is called **reinforced bending**. Add more leverage by pushing down with your thumb on the back of the neck.

## 85 Twang It!

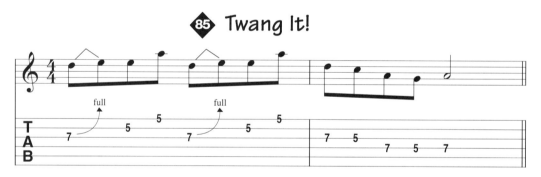

You can also bend up and back down. Simply bend up, then release the pressure slowly. Sounds cool, huh?

## 86 Up and Down

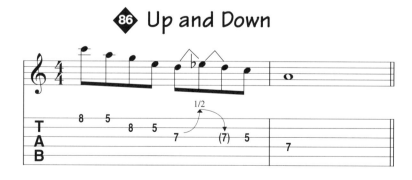

Don't bend too much, or you'll be buying a new string!

# LESSON 9
## *Strike up the band...*

**A**s in the first book, this last section isn't a lesson...it's your jam session!

All the **FastTrack**™ books (Guitar, Keyboard, Bass and Drums) have the same last section. This way, you can either play by yourself along with the CD or form a band with your friends.

So, whether the band's on the CD or in your garage, let the show begin...

**87** **88** **Nervous**

full band / minus guitar

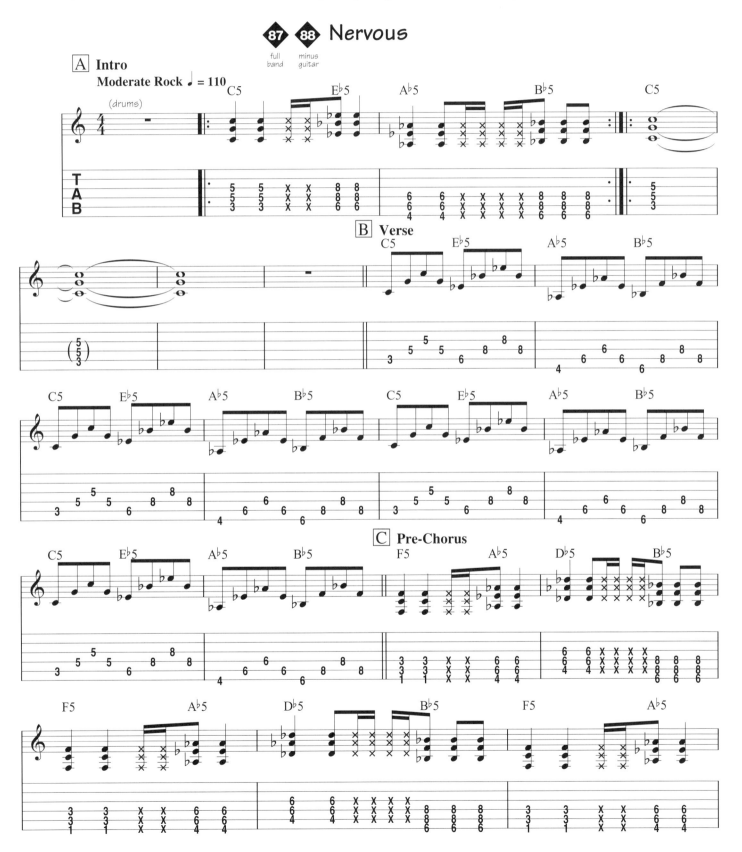

43

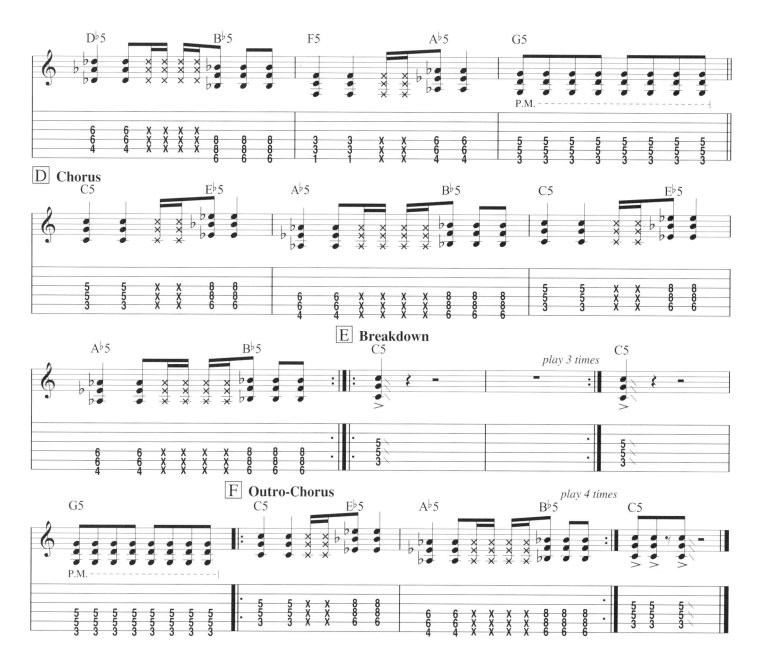

## Basement Jam

**89** full band  **90** minus guitar

### A Intro
**Moderate Rock/Shuffle** ♩ = 136

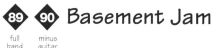

### ℈ B Melody

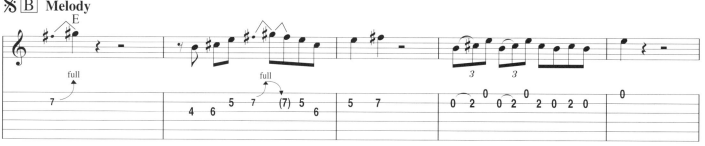

# Dim the Lights

We would be sad that this was the end of our relationship,
but we'll see you again in **FastTrack**™ **Guitar Songbook 2.**

# A FAREWELL GIFT

## *(...it's the least we could do!)*

We expect you to use the entire book as a reference, but this has now become a tradition—a "cheat sheet" with all the notes and chords you learned. Don't forget to practice often!

## Notes in Fifth Position:

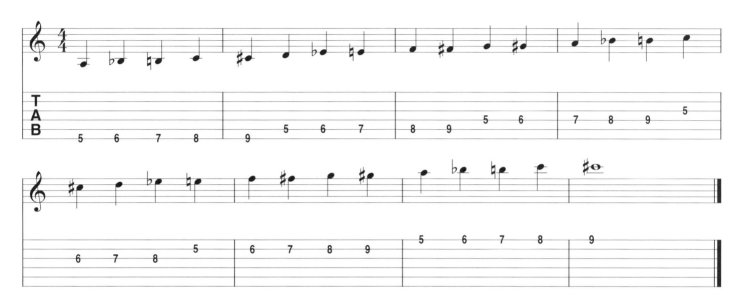

## Chords and Shapes:

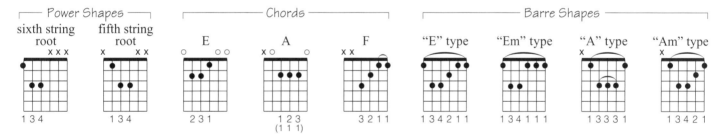

## What's next?

You've started to master the guitar in just a short time, but where do you go now?

 **Practice, practice, practice.** What more can we say but practice every day?

 Buy **FastTrack™ Guitar Songbooks 1** and **2**, featuring rock score format of hits from Eric Clapton, The Beatles, Elton John, and many more.

 Buy **FastTrack™ Guitar Chords & Scales**, an excellent reference book with over 1,400 guitar chords and voicings, patterns for eight scales and seven modes, and a special "Jam Session" with popular chord progressions.

 **Enjoy what you do.** If you don't enjoy what you're doing, there's no sense in doing it.

Bye for now...

# SONG INDEX

## (...gotta have one!)